TRENDS IN SOUTHEAST ASIA

PUBLIC PERCEPTIONS OF THE ELECTION COMMISSION, ELECTION MANAGEMENT AND DEMOCRACY IN MALAYSIA

Helen Ting M.H. and
Andrew Kam Jia Yi

ISSUE

19

2021

YUSOF ISHAK
INSTITUTE

Published by: ISEAS Publishing
                 30 Heng Mui Keng Terrace
                 Singapore 119614
                 publish@iseas.edu.sg
                 http://bookshop.iseas.edu.sg

ISEAS Library Cataloguing-in-Publication Data

Name(s): Ting, Helen, 1964–, author. | Kam, Andrew Jia Yi, 1979–, author.
Title: Public perceptions of the Election Commission, election management and democracy in Malaysia / by Helen Ting M.H. and Andrew Kam Jia Yi.
Description: Singapore : ISEAS-Yusof Ishak Institute, November 2021. | Series: Trends in Southeast Asia, ISSN 0219-3213 ; TRS19/21 | Includes bibliographical references.
Identifiers: ISBN 9789815011173 (soft cover) | ISBN 9789815011180 (pdf)
Subjects: LCSH: Elections—Malaysia—Public opinion. | Malaysia—Election Commission—Public opinion. | Public institutions—Malaysia—Public opinion.
Classification: LCC DS501 I59T no. 19(2021)

Typeset by Superskill Graphics Pte Ltd
Printed in Singapore by Mainland Press Pte Ltd

FOREWORD

The economic, political, strategic and cultural dynamism in Southeast Asia has gained added relevance in recent years with the spectacular rise of giant economies in East and South Asia. This has drawn greater attention to the region and to the enhanced role it now plays in international relations and global economics.

The sustained effort made by Southeast Asian nations since 1967 towards a peaceful and gradual integration of their economies has had indubitable success, and perhaps as a consequence of this, most of these countries are undergoing deep political and social changes domestically and are constructing innovative solutions to meet new international challenges. Big Power tensions continue to be played out in the neighbourhood despite the tradition of neutrality exercised by the Association of Southeast Asian Nations (ASEAN).

The **Trends in Southeast Asia** series acts as a platform for serious analyses by selected authors who are experts in their fields. It is aimed at encouraging policymakers and scholars to contemplate the diversity and dynamism of this exciting region.

THE EDITORS

Series Chairman:
   Choi Shing Kwok

Series Editor:
   Ooi Kee Beng

Editorial Committee:
   Daljit Singh
   Francis E. Hutchinson
   Norshahril Saat

Public Perceptions of the Election Commission, Election Management and Democracy in Malaysia

By Helen Ting M.H. and Andrew Kam Jia Yi

EXECUTIVE SUMMARY

- This report presents findings from a nationwide face-to-face survey of 2,627 Malaysians between March and April 2021 regarding public perceptions on the Election Commission (EC) and on election management.
- Malaysians by and large hold a cautious, moderate affirmation of the state of democracy in Malaysia, and of it having made notable progress over the past decade.
- A quarter of respondents regard the 2018 general election to be very free or/and fair, while 43 per cent think that it was free/fair though not without problems. This perception appears to have been influenced by the fact that there was a change of federal government.
- Public confidence in the integrity and impartiality of the election management process and the EC is weakly affirmative, as revealed by a majority expressing a lack of confidence in an eventual online voting system being handled transparently.
- Urban residents generally have greater distrust in state institutions.
- Some notable contrasts in regional trends:
  - Sarawakians have a high level of trust in state institutions.
  - Sabahans have the lowest appreciation for the progress made in the state of democracy in the country, the lowest satisfaction with civil liberty, or the lowest trust in state institutions except for the Malaysian Anti-Corruption Commission (MACC) and the EC.

- West Malaysians have the lowest level of trust in the MACC and EC but express the highest level of appreciation for the progress that have made in the state of democracy.

Public Perceptions of the Election Commission, Election Management and Democracy in Malaysia

By Helen Ting M.H. and Andrew Kam Jia Yi[1]

INTRODUCTION

A lot have been published on the subject of democracy in Malaysia, yet there are few comprehensive survey-based academic studies on how Malaysians view the state of democracy, and, even rarer, in relation to election management and the country's Election Commission (EC). Welsh (1996) on political attitudes among Malaysians in 1994 was one such study and based on a survey of 400 respondents, while the study by Muhammad Fathi Yusof et al. (2015) on public perception towards the EC is based on a small survey of seven questions among 1,104 respondents in 2014/15. Periodic and systematic international surveys on democracy have been conducted by the Asian Barometer of Democracy surveys, and Malaysia has been included since 2007 during its Second Wave Asian Barometer Survey (ABS). Thus far, three working papers or report with a focus on Malaysia have been produced from the ABS (Welsh, Suffian and Aeria 2007; Welsh Suffian and Aeria 2008; Welsh 2014). Otherwise, outputs from ABS have been in the form of cross-country regional studies among several Asian countries which include Malaysia (Chang, Chu and

[1] Helen Ting Mu Hung (PhD, ScPo Paris) and Andrew Kam Jia Yi (PhD, ANU) are both associate professors and senior research fellows at the Institute of Malaysian and International Studies (IKMAS), Universiti Kebangsaan Malaysia (UKM).

1

Welsh 2013, Chu, Welsh and Chang 2013, Huang, Chu and Chang 2013; Ikeda 2013; Lu 2013; Mujani and Liddle 2013; Park 2013; Wang and Tan 2013; Chu and Welsh 2015; Kang and Lee 2018). While cross-country comparative studies are useful in contextualizing political perception in Malaysia within an international context, they do not provide a detailed understanding of Malaysians' perceptions on the EC and other state institutions, the management of elections, and the state of democracy.

This report is an analysis of the findings from a nationwide survey conducted with 2,627 respondents between March and April 2021. The objectives are to find out how Malaysian citizens evaluate the performance of the EC in managing elections, perceive the neutrality of the EC, and also how they perceive the state of democracy and of political authorities in the country. As the EC is one of the fundamental institutions in the operationalization of democracy, i.e., in conducting popular elections, public perception of its performance and function is best understood in the general context of the latter's evaluation of the state of democracy and perception of the legitimacy of state institutions as a whole. Hence, besides aspects related strictly to the management of elections, the survey casts its net wider to gather the views of the respondents on the state of democracy in the country as a means of providing some context to their views. Focus group discussions were carried out before the survey to gather preliminary information on the perspectives of people from a variety of background and profiles. The questionnaire was formulated with that knowledge as the base.

CONCEPTUAL FRAMEWORK AND POLITICAL CONTEXT

To analyse the survey results, this report constructs a conceptual framework adapted from the works of David Easton (1975) and Pippa Norris (2011). Norris (2011) is a cross-country study of citizens' perception of democracy and the legitimacy of the governments of their respective countries. The idea of political support can have many shades of meaning. It can be directed at different components of a political system and is hence multidimensional. Easton develops the concept of political support and proposes to distinguish between what he sees as "specific" support from "diffuse" support which is qualitatively different in several aspects. By "specific support", he refers to the satisfaction of the public with the "perceived outputs and performance of the political authorities" (Easton 1975, p. 437). Hence specific support is directed at a specified object, at their "outputs", i.e., the "perceived decisions, policies, actions, utterances or the general style of these authorities" (p. 437). Specific support is more changeable over time, since it is related to the ongoing performance of the political authorities. The gauging of public support for the government of the day in opinion polls, for instance, fits into this understanding.

Diffuse support, on the other hand, evolves more slowly, and is relatively independent of the short-term performance and outputs of the political objects. It is more basic in nature, indicating some form of "attachment to political objects for their own sake", "evaluations of what an object is or represents" and "not of what it does" (Easton 1975, pp. 444, 445). Diffuse support is usually based on goodwill accumulated over time from prolonged beneficial outputs the political object has produced. On the other hand, a perceived deterioration of performance from the political object over enough length of time may erode diffuse support.

Diffuse support typically expresses itself in two forms: trust, and belief in the legitimacy of political objects. Hence one conceptual distinction between diffuse and specific support lies with the expression of *trust* or confidence in the integrity of the institutions for the former as opposed to the approval based on satisfaction with ongoing *performance* for the latter. Secondly, diffuse support is typically directed at more abstract objects such as democratic principles or its general workings (denoted as "regime" by Easton), while specific support is more relevant to specific political actors, such as elected office-holders.

Building on the works of Easton, Norris (2011) develops her conceptual framework of "systems support" to explore citizens' level of political support towards the nation-state, political authorities and actors. She examines five dimensions of support, namely the national community, the general regime principles, the overall performance of the regime, confidence in state institutions and trust in elected and appointed officeholders. This survey does not intend to adopt her framework, but it shares the understanding in Norris (2011) to treat the concepts of diffuse and specific support as being situated on a continuum rather than as two distinct types of political support (see Figure 1).

In this report, we deal with two categories of political objects: The political authorities and the regime. "Political authorities" is defined as "those who are responsible for the day-to-day actions taken in the name of a political system" (Easton 1975, p. 437) while the more abstract concept of "regime" is understood as "the underlying order of political life" (p. 436). Among the types of political authority, we additionally distinguish between "partisan" and "non-partisan" institutions (Huang, Lee, and Lin 2013); it has been found that people's trust in partisan institutions, as opposed to non-partisan ones, are influenced by their political affiliation.

Institutions such as the Parliament or the Executive are constituted through partisan elections and are denoted as "partisan institutions", whereas state institutions such as the civil service, the judiciary or the police force are categorized as "non-partisan". Since incumbent office-holders such as the prime minister and the government of the day are appointed based on partisan majority in the parliament, it is not unreasonable to anticipate that satisfaction of their performance may be subject to partisan evaluation. This means that supporters of the parties or coalition forming the government may evaluate the office-holders more favourably than the supporters of the opposition parties or coalition. Huang, Lee and Lin (2013) argue that citizens are frequently bombarded with information that challenges their "partisan cognitions" and often people "may rely on their partisanship as a heuristic shortcut in evaluating the trustworthiness of partisan institutions" (p. 48). In this sense, such asymmetric manifestation of trust may be explained by increased partisan polarization.

On the other hand, state institutions such as the police, the judiciary and the Malaysian Anti-Corruption Commission (MACC) are expected to be politically neutral. Hence, they would theoretically be evaluated on less equivocal grounds or without being swayed by partisan attachment. While governments may come and go (which was not the case in Malaysia at the federal level before 2018, but has since become so), the functioning of other state institutions are supposed to be more stable

Figure 1: Conceptual Framework: Public Support and Perception of the Political System

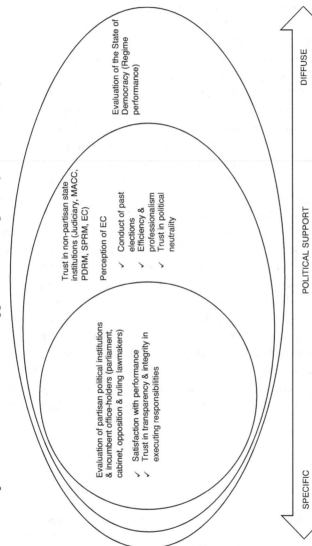

Evaluation of partisan political institutions & incumbent office-holders (parliament, cabinet, opposition & ruling lawmakers)

✓ Satisfaction with performance
✓ Trust in transparency & integrity in executing responsibilities

Trust in non-partisan state institutions (Judiciary, MACC, PDRM, SPRM, EC)

Perception of EC

✓ Conduct of past elections
✓ Efficiency & professionalism
✓ Trust in political neutrality

Evaluation of the State of Democracy (Regime performance)

SPECIFIC   POLITICAL SUPPORT   DIFFUSE

and neutral, and cannot be changed overnight. In effect, any attempt at reforming state institutions would also take time. Huang, Lee and Lin (2013) nonetheless found that distrust may also exist in some supposedly "neutral" institutions, which they explain as possibly arising from bad governance rather than partisan polarization.

The EC is expected to be a non-partisan institution but has been criticized by the opposition and civil society actors as being biased in favour of the ruling government.[2] The conduct of the 2018 general election was also subjected to a litany of criticisms, ranging from the contentious way the pre-electoral boundary redelimitation exercise was conducted, the choice of a weekday for the poll, the cutting out of the picture of Dr Mahathir from election posters of the opposition coalition, Pakatan Harapan (PH), to the refusal of a number of presiding officers of polling stations to sign Form 14 to certify the final results of the vote count.[3] Shortly after the last general election in 2018 (GE14), the Coalition for Clean and Fair Elections (BERSIH 2.0), the country's electoral reform movement, issued a press statement urging the new PH government to "act immediately to restore public confidence in the Election Commission" (BERSIH 2018). It pushed for the resignation of the entire EC line-up based on the "blatant evidence of all the frauds and mismanagement" they had gathered before and during GE14. It also urged the government to set up a tribunal in accordance with the federal constitution to investigate their alleged wrongdoings for failing to conduct GE14 in a clean and fair manner. In the same statement, BERSIH 2.0 also urged the government to set up a Royal Commission of Inquiry (RCI) on Elections to "investigate any possible criminal misconduct, fraud, or

---

[2] See, for example, "Azmin: Rulers Rejected Proposed Appointment of Najib's Aide in EC", *Malaysiakini*, 4 November 2016; "Ex-EC chief admits to gerrymandering?", Malaysiakini, 25 November 2013.

[3] "Minister: Refusal to Sign Form 14 Should Not Have Happened", *Malaysiakini*, 6 September 2018.

violation of election laws". Soon after, the EC chairman announced his resignation following the shortening of his tenure, while the rest of the EC members departed towards the end of 2018 after the establishment of a tribunal was announced. Instead of an RCI, the government set up an Electoral Reform Committee to conduct a comprehensive review of all aspects of election management and laws governing them as well as the electoral system, based on international standards and inputs from stakeholders.

Scholars have documented how successive ruling governments attempted to interfere in election management or curtail the autonomy of the EC over time (see, e.g., Rachagan 1993; Lim 2002, 2005; Chacko 2019). A sympathetic view of the role of the EC is offered by Rachagan (1993), which notes that, "In defence of the Commission it may be said that the Commission has to work within the law and the laws currently allow the Commission to be dictated to by the party in power" (p. 48). Levitsky and Way (2010) categorize Malaysia as a "competitive authoritarian" regime, which recognizes that while its elections were genuinely competitive, they were not totally free and never fair. There was no level playing field, as the ruling government would exploit to the fullest its "incumbency advantage" to ensure its electoral victories.

Notable in this context is that while the EC should be held accountable for its election management, it is not empowered to act on many of the unacceptable electoral practices during the election campaign. For instance, an EC officer has no power to take action on election offences except to refer the alleged wrongdoings to the police and MACC. It does not even have a final say on the constituency delineation plan it is tasked to prepare. The electoral reform movement initiated by BERSIH had been pushing for reforms for over a decade to render the EC more autonomous and effective in the conduct of cleaner and fairer elections. The election observation report prepared by election watchdogs also highlighted the problematic fact that the EC Chair then had worked for nine years as personal aide to a leading UMNO politician prior to being appointed to the EC (PEMANTAU 2018). In September 2018, a well-known lawyer, Azhar Azizan Harun, was appointed the new EC Chair, followed by the appointment of new commissioners. Civil society leaders welcomed their appointment as a number of them were known to be vocal on issues related to electoral reform, including one who was previously an activist involved with BERSIH 2.0. The chairperson of BERSIH 2.0, Thomas Fann, acknowledged notable proactive efforts under Azhar Harun to make election management more transparent and responsive to stakeholders' grievances (Fann 2019). Hence it would have been interesting to examine public perception of the EC within this context. The fall of the PH government in February 2020 however has complicated the interpretation of survey results as there has since been a change of the EC chairperson.

In this survey, we propose to analyse political support for three political objects, from the more general to the more specific, namely: regime performance in terms of the state of democracy; level of trust in non-partisan state institutions; and lastly, trust in partisan political institutions and satisfaction with the performance of office-holders. The evaluation of the EC will be more detailed and is contextualized within the second component.

One caveat to add here is that it is important to distinguish public perception of democracy and political support from a rigorous academic assessment based on criteria in accordance with an ideal, normative concept of democracy. In other words, a popular government is not necessarily synonymous with a more democratic government. As well acknowledged in some scholarly works, an authoritarian country may enjoy a higher level of popular support than a democratic one (Kotzian 2010; Norris 2011; Chang, Chu and Welsh 2013). The second and third waves of Asian Barometer Surveys (ABS II and III) between 2005 and 2012, for instance, found that a one-party regime such as Vietnam enjoyed the highest institutional support above other Southeast Asian countries such as Indonesia, the Philippines, Malaysia, Thailand and Singapore (Chang, Chu and Welsh 2013). The cross-country study of Norris (2011) based on World Values Survey 2005–7 similarly found that autocratic countries such as Vietnam, China and Iran enjoyed higher institutional confidence than electoral or liberal democracies (pp. 100, 111).

Various explanations of this paradox between strong subjective institutional support and shortfall in normative democratic features in some countries have been advanced, including pre-emptive measures taken by authoritarian governments to suppress voices of dissent and opposition as well as independent news media, and authoritarian political disposition of the public (Norris 2011; Chang, Chu and Welsh 2013). Kotzian (2010) found in a study of thirty-six countries that economic performance constitutes the most important determinant in explaining public support.

A process of democratization may engender rising aspiration for a more substantive democratic style of governance and an ideal form of government, a standard which may not be fulfilled by the actual workings of the political reality in the country. This disparity in expectation and performance among an emergent critical mass of "critical citizens" may lead to more frustration, disappointment and backlash in a country undergoing democratization, leading to a more critical assessment of the state of democracy by the citizens of a country than citizens of an autocratic country who have tempered their political expectations. Norris (2011) calls this gap between rising aspiration and disappointment with democratic practices as "democratic deficit". Hence a more positive attitude towards the political authorities may simply be due to congruence between expectation and reality, and not the consequence of a more democratic approach in governance.

Based on ABS II and III, Chang, Chu and Welsh (2013) found that the substantial confidence of citizens in state institutions in most Southeast Asian countries was associated with the perception that their governance was "effective and marked by integrity" (p. 162). Chang, Chu and Welsh (2013) also note that Malaysia and Singapore, despite being assessed as less democratic than Indonesia and the Philippines, have been found to be more effective in controlling corruption and upholding the rule of law than the latter, according to the Worldwide Governance Indicators of World Bank (p. 155).

In any case, regardless of whether they are based on an accurate perception of reality, political legitimacy and public confidence are vital for the optimal and effective functioning of a political system. In a democratic system, ensuring that citizens elect their own representatives through a free and fair conduct of election is fundamental to political legitimacy and more so in Malaysia, where general elections have been held regularly since independence. In effect, impartial management and effective monitoring of all stages of a general election are crucial if the electoral outcome is to be regarded by both sides of the political divide as credible and acceptable. Serious disputes over election outcomes without an effective and impartial mechanism of deliberation could degenerate into civil unrest, as had happened in Myanmar recently and other countries.

SURVEY METHODS AND DEMOGRAPHIC PROFILE OF RESPONDENTS

The survey targeted 2,400 respondents, with sampling units being divided into three regions: West Malaysia (1,600 respondents), Sabah (400 respondents), and Sarawak (400 respondents). Sampling sizes of Sabah and Sarawak were increased to take into account the representation of the more diverse ethnic composition in the two states. The survey used stratified random sampling technique based on the 2010 Census data from the Department of Statistics Malaysia, with a 2 per cent margin of error and a confidence level of 95 per cent. The sampling was stratified based on the population size and ethnic composition of each district.

A pilot study was conducted in February 2021 before a full, face-to-face survey was conducted in stages throughout Malaysia in March and April 2021. A total of forty enumerators were involved in the data collection process using handphones and keying in responses directly into the questionnaire set up online while the interviews took place.[4] In view of the COVID-19 pandemic, face-to-face interviews were conducted with strict adherence to the standard operating procedures (SOP) announced from time to time by the Ministry of Health. Data collection was also conducted online through self-administered approach

---

[4] Depending on the land use of each district (commercial, residential, rural), the enumerators recruited their respondents in different locations based on the number and profile of sampling as defined for each district.

in areas difficult to access, or to overcome movement restriction orders.[5] When necessary, the questionnaire was also printed out and filled in physically for the enumerators to key into the online system afterwards. The enumerators resorted to this approach whenever the broadband connection was unstable.

Table 1 shows the profile of respondents collected based on the proposed regional units of sampling. The survey sample collected exceeds the planned sample size and totals 2,627 respondents with 1,657 from West Malaysia, 506 from Sabah, and 464 from Sarawak. Malays constitute almost 48 per cent of the total, followed by 21 per cent Chinese and 6.1 per cent Indians. The ethnic groups in Sabah and Sarawak are more heterogeneous and therefore only the largest groups are reported in the table. Smaller groups are subsumed under "Other Bumi" categories. An important caveat is that the Malays are over-represented in Sabah while the Chinese are under-represented in Sarawak.

The demographic profile of the respondents is as shown in Table 2. Balanced gender representation as well as their distribution in each region have been ensured. Respondents are almost equally distributed in urban (34 per cent), semi-urban (33 per cent), and rural (33 per cent) areas. We have classified districts under Majlis Bandaraya (City Council) as "urban", Majlis Perbandaran (Municipal Council) as "semi-urban and the rest as "rural". 80 per cent of the respondents in West Malaysia live in urban and semi-urban areas (44 per cent urban and 36 per cent semi-urban) while there are more rural respondents in Sabah (55 per cent) and Sarawak (53 per cent). The table also shows that except for Sarawak,

---

[5] In this case, respondents with the required profiles and number were obtained through contacts in the districts or the phone number database of the survey agency. This approach was also used when there were difficulties in recruiting sufficient Chinese respondents from Johor and Melaka during the fieldwork. Potential respondents were first contacted via telephone to seek their consent, and once they had agreed, the Internet link for the online questionnaire would be sent to them to fill. The enumerator would be on standby to provide further clarification on specific questions. The self-administered approach was least preferred as incompletely filled questionnaires would be rejected.

Table 1: Profile of Respondents by Region and Ethnicity

		West Malaysia	Sabah	Sarawak	Malaysia
Malay	N	1,072	40	139	1,251
	%	64.7	7.9	30.0	47.6
Chinese	N	416	47	97	560
	%	25.1	9.3	20.9	21.3
Indian	N	160			160
	%	9.7			6.1
Kadazandusun-Murut	N		166		166
	%		32.8		6.3
Bajau-Suluk	N		118		118
	%		23.3		4.5
Other Bumi (Sabah)	N		118		118
	%		23.3		4.5
Iban	N			130	130
	%			28.0	4.9
Melanau	N			52	52
	%			11.2	2.0
Other Bumi (Sarawak)	N			45	45
	%			9.7	1.7
Others	N	9	17	1	27
	%	0.5	3.4	0.2	1.0
Total (by region)	N	1,657	506	464	2,627
	%	100	100	100	100

Table 2: Demographic Profile of Respondents

		Malaysia		West Malaysia		Sabah		Sarawak	
		Frequency	%	Frequency	%	Frequency	%	Frequency	%
1. Gender	Male	1,327	50.5	832	50.2	259	51.2	236	50.9
	Female	1,300	49.5	825	49.8	247	48.8	228	49.1
	Total	2,627	100.0	1,657	100.0	506	100.0	464	100.0
2. Age (in years)	18–20	281	10.7	171	10.3	52	10.3	58	12.5
	21–24	498	19	341	20.6	92	18.2	65	14.0
	25–29	447	17	333	20.1	57	11.3	57	12.3
	30–34	366	13.9	256	15.4	70	13.8	40	8.6
	35–39	252	9.6	159	9.6	62	12.3	31	6.7
	40–44	178	6.8	91	5.5	52	10.3	35	7.5
	45–49	139	5.3	65	3.9	33	6.5	41	8.8
	50–54	137	5.2	75	4.5	23	4.5	39	8.4
	55–59	107	4.1	54	3.3	20	4.0	33	7.1
	> 60	222	8.5	112	6.8	45	8.9	65	14.0
	Total	2,627	100.0	1,657	100.0	506	100.0	464	100.0
3. Area	Urban	903	34.4	727	43.9	104	20.6	72	15.5
	Semi-Urban	862	32.8	594	35.8	123	24.3	145	31.3
	Rural	862	32.8	336	20.3	279	55.1	247	53.2
	Total	2,627	100.0	1,657	100.0	506	100.0	464	100.0

more than 60 per cent are between 18 and 34 years of age. For Sarawak, more than 60 per cent are aged between 18 and 39. Those between 21 and 24 years old constitute the largest age group in all the three regions. Table 3 gives an idea of who these young respondents (aged 18–24 years) are: 60.6 per cent are still students, while 20.5 per cent are in entry or non-managerial positions in private companies. About 39.9 per cent of those holding STPM certificate or below are no longer studying and mostly working, and half of them work in lower-level company positions.

Figure 2 shows that the respondents also comprise mostly of the bottom 40 per cent of the national income bracket[6] (B40) groups. 80.4 per cent of the respondents reported a monthly household income of RM4,999 and below. Sabah and Sarawak samples have a higher proportion of the B40 respondents, i.e., 87 per cent for Sabah and 86 per cent for Sarawak, whereas 77 per cent of respondents from West Malaysia are in this category.

In terms of main occupation, respondents are mainly employees in the private sector, self-employed or business owners (see Figure 3). Almost 20 per cent are students. In terms of educational level (Figure 4), 35 per cent are SPM holders or equivalent. Half of the respondents have qualifications above SPM-level. 10.4 per cent holds a STPM certificate while 21.0 per cent of respondents hold a diploma. A further 17.1 per cent hold a bachelor's degree and a small 2.5 per cent hold a degree or a postgraduate degree as their highest level of education.

POLITICAL AWARENESS AND KNOWLEDGE OF RESPONDENTS

To assess the political awareness of the respondents, the questionnaire gathered information on the principal means of access to and the key sources of information on politics and current affairs which the

---

[6] The Department of Statistics Malaysia defined B40 as the lower income group with monthly incomes below RM4,850. The 40 per cent of the middle-income group, M40, have incomes range between RM4,851 and RM10,970 while the top 20 per cent of the high income T20 have incomes above RM10,971.

Table 3: Occupation and Academic Qualification (18–24 years old)

Main Occupation	Highest Academic Qualification					Total (Occupation)
	Postgraduate	Degree	Diploma	STPM	SPM or Below	
Student	3	74	86	81	228	472
Public Sector	0	4	2	2	7	15
Private sector (Professional/ Management)	1	5	19	2	6	33
Private sector (employee)	0	6	43	17	94	160
Doing business	0	1	5	4	16	26
Self-employed	0	5	8	8	25	46
Unemployed	1	0	2	6	18	27
Total	5	95	165	120	394	779

Figure 2: Monthly Household Income by Region

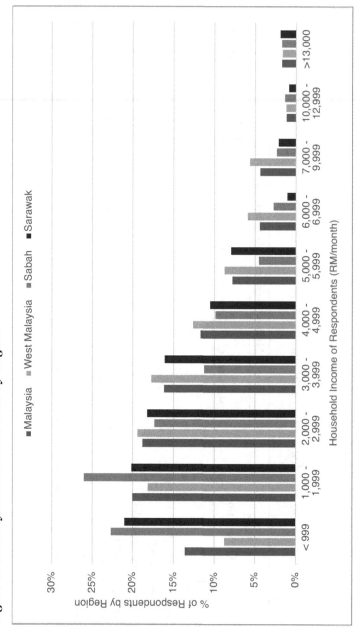

Figure 3: Employment Status

Figure 4: Highest Level of Education

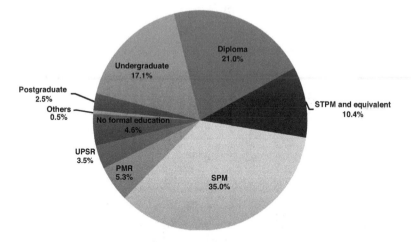

Table 4: How Often Do You Follow News Related to Politics and Government?

	Frequency	%
1. Every day	235	8.9
2. A few times a week	587	22.3
3. Once or twice a week	878	33.4
4. Never	870	33.1
5. Others	57	2.2
Total	2,627	100.0

respondents relied on. Table 4 raises a few concerns because nearly one-third of the respondents never follow news related to politics and government. Another one-third merely follow news once or twice a week. The sources of news are shown in Figure 5.

Figure 5 shows that television still plays an important role in disseminating political information. This is followed by social media, i.e., Facebook, Twitter and Instagram. Printed newspapers and digital platforms such as WhatsApp, WeChat, and Telegram trail behind as the next most important access to information on current affairs. An analysis

Figure 5: Means of Access to Political Information

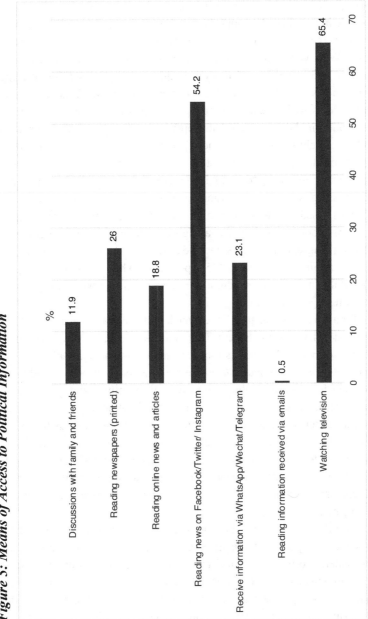

by region (Table 5) found a similar trend, with some notable variations in relative importance. The importance of television as the medium to learn about current affairs becomes even more dominant in Sabah and Sarawak, but in West Malaysia, this is rivalled by social media such as Facebook, Twitter, and Instagram on an almost equal footing. In addition, reading online news and blogs constitutes an important way for West Malaysian respondents to be kept informed politically (23 per cent). In Sabah, electronic media such as WhatsApp/WeChat/Telegram (23.1 per cent) follow closely behind printed newspapers as the fourth most important suppliers of political news, just as the case is in West Malaysia. West Malaysians appear to have slightly more varied and spread-out means of accessing political information compared to the other two regions. An analysis based on the urban/rural divide reflects a similar overall pattern in terms though it also reveals a slightly different variation of strength. Unsurprisingly, online news and blogs remain an important channel of current affairs for urbanites (25.2 per cent), while printed newspapers constitute an important medium to access political news among "semi-urbanites" (30.2 per cent).

Figure 6 details the main TV channels and newspapers accessed by the respondents. Many cite Buletin TV3, Astro Awani, and TV2 as their main sources of political news. As for the printed newspapers, *Berita Harian*, *Sinar Harian* and *Harian Metro* are the most popular ones. In addition to being less informed about news related to politics and government, respondents appear to be quite uninterested in attending political talks; only a quarter stated that they had attended one. 14 per cent say they were involved in an election campaign. Although the numbers are low, it is interesting to note that compared with other regions, Sabah respondents seem more politically engaged. Table 6 provides a regional breakdown of the profile of the respondents in terms of political awareness or engagement.

In order to assess whether the respondents are well informed about how the EC operates, three statements about the EC were posed to the respondents to mark as "true" or "false", or "unsure". Figure 7 shows how more than a quarter of them admit that they are "unsure". It is found that only 24.1 per cent are aware that the EC "does not have the full authority to monitor, investigate and indict any parties who violate the

Table 5: Main Means of Access to Political News and Current Affairs (by Region and Urban/Rural)

		Region			Urban/Semi-Urban/Rural		
		W. Malaysia	Sabah	Sarawak	Urban	Semi-Urban	Rural
Television	%	57.5	81.4	77.8	58.9	62.9	75.5
Printed newspapers	%	25.7	24.5	29.1	21.6	30.2	26.6
Online news & blogs	%	23.1	12.3	10.6	25.0	18.9	12.0
Facebook/Twitter/Instagram	%	57.3	46.6	51.1	58.5	50.4	53.4
WhatsApp/WeChat/Telegram	%	24.2	23.1	19.0	22.2	23.1	24.0
Friends and family	%	12.1	11.3	11.9	13.4	14.2	8.0
Total	N	3,314	1,012	928	1,806	1,724	1,724
	%	200	200	200	200	200	200

Note: Respondents were asked to provide two major means of access to news related to current affairs and political development in the country.

Figure 6: Sources of Political News and Current Affairs

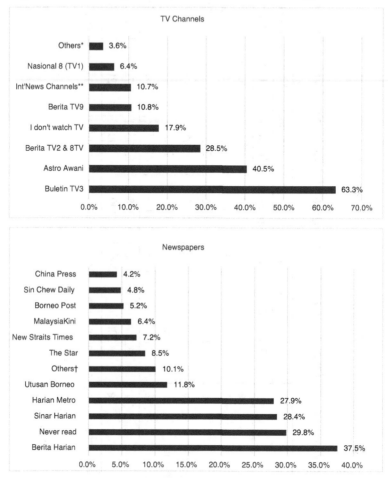

Notes:

*Include *Berita AlHijrah*, etc.

**Include Al-Jazeera, BBC and CNN.

†Those with 1.5 per cent or less readership, including *The Sun, Makkai Osai, Daily Express, Harakah, Free Malaysia Today, The Edge, The Malaysia Insight, Malaysia Namban, Oriental Daily, Malay Mail*.

Table 6: Engagements in Election Campaign and Political Talks

1. Have you attended any political talks before?

		Region			
		West Malaysia	Sabah	Sarawak	Total
Yes	Total	351	178	125	654
	% within region	21.2%	35.2%	26.9%	24.9%
No	Total	1,306	328	339	1,973
	% within region	78.8%	64.8%	73.1%	75.1%
Total	Total	1,657	506	464	2,627
	% within region	100.0%	100.0%	100.0%	100.0%

2. Have you ever been involved in an election campaign?

		West Malaysia	Sabah	Sarawak	Total
Yes	Total	184	111	74	369
	% within region	11.1%	21.9%	15.9%	14.0%
No	Total	1,473	395	390	2,258
	% within region	88.9%	78.1%	84.1%	86.0%
Total	Total	1,657	506	464	2,627
	% within region	100.0%	100.0%	100.0%	100.0%

Figure 7: Knowledge on the Election Commission

The Election Commission does not have full authority to monitor, investigate and indict any parties who violate the election laws

26.1% 24.1% 49.9%

■ TRUE
■ FALSE
■ Unsure

The Election Commission has no power to audit and monitor the financial expenditures of political parties in the election campaign

29.0% 33.3% 37.7%

The appointment of the Election Commission Chairman requires bipartisan support (ie support of both the ruling and opposition MPs) of the Parliament.

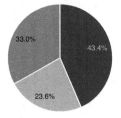

33.0% 43.4% 23.6%

election laws". On the lack of power for the EC to "audit and monitor the financial expenditures of political parties in the election campaign", about a third got it right. On the other hand, 43.4 per cent of the respondents thought that the appointment of the EC chairperson requires the support of both the government and the opposition members of the parliament! Overall, 30 per cent of the respondents got one answer right, 20 per cent responded correctly to two questions, and only 3.6 per cent managed to get all the three answers right. This demonstrates that much of the public perception of the EC may be based on inadequate knowledge of how elections are conducted as well as what falls under the responsibilities of the EC and what does not.

PERCEPTION OF THE STATE OF DEMOCRACY

This section examines public perception of the state of democracy in Malaysia. Two sets of questions are posed. The first consists of three queries asking the respondents to rate the state of democracy on a scale of 1 to 7 as of today, as it was ten years ago and their anticipation of it in ten years' time. The three questions also capture a sense of whether they perceive the situation as improving and whether they are optimistic of the country's democratic future. The second set of questions ask the respondents to rate their level of satisfaction with the state of media freedom, freedom of expression, association and assembly. As civil liberties are important aspects to ensure the health of democracy, the two sets of indicators provide us with an idea of how the respondents evaluate the state of democracy in the country.

(a) Perceived State of Democracy

As seen from Table 7, Malaysians generally perceive that the state of democracy in Malaysia has made some advancement when compared to ten years ago and will make further progress in the ten years to come.

Table 7: Perceived State of Democracy

• Is Malaysia a democratic country? On a scale of 1 to 7, please indicate your assessment of the current state of democracy in Malaysia. • How was the level of democracy in Malaysia ten years ago? • Where do you expect the state of democracy in Malaysia to be in ten years' time? *(1 signifies "very undemocratic" and 7 signifies "very democratic")*					
	N	**Mean**	**Median**	**Mode**	**Std. Dev.**
Today	2,627	4.90	5	5	1.356
10 years ago	2,627	4.61	5	5	1.539
10 years to come	2,627	5.02	5	5	1.501

Nonetheless, the smaller standard deviation suggests that there is a greater consensus over the assessment of the state of democracy today than the assessment about it ten years ago or in the future. On the other hand, the mode and median values for all three responses are 5 out of 7, which is just one point above the mid-point of the scale, 4. If we understand 4 as an expression of scepticism or aloofness which is neither positive nor negative, 5 would be a conservative and cautious affirmation in a slightly positive light towards the future state of democracy in the country. Malaysians seem to think that democratic progress in the next ten years will be much more challenging when compared with the progress that has been achieved over the past ten years (given the very small increase in the mean value for the future from "today").

The superimposed graph in Figure 8 compare the perceived state of democracy among the regions. West Malaysians seem to be the most upbeat about the extent of democratic improvement over the past ten years. They affirm a greater extent of democratization over the past ten years and anticipate Malaysia to achieve a higher state of democracy in the ten years to come than the other two regions. Sabahans only see a very slight improvement in democracy over the last ten years and appear to be the most dissatisfied with the state of democracy among the three. They are also the least unanimous about how the state of democracy will improve in the next decade or so, given the higher value of standard deviation and with a mode value of 7 (not shown). The perception of Sarawakians is situated in between the two regions.

With the benefit of hindsight, follow-up questions to the respondents to provide reasons for their responses should have been added so as to get a clearer idea of why they had evaluated the state of democracy the way they did, which unfortunately was not done. Hence there is no way to find out why they answered the way they did. We offer here a speculative interpretation of these contrasting regional views based on the electoral outcomes during the 2018 general election (GE14) and the 2020 Sabah state election.

During GE14, there was a significant vote swing against the incumbent in West Malaysia, while election results in Sabah were quite divided, resulting in a tied situation. Rural voters in Sarawak, on the other hand, were almost solidly behind the political status quo. As the

Figure 8: Perceived State of Democracy (by Region)

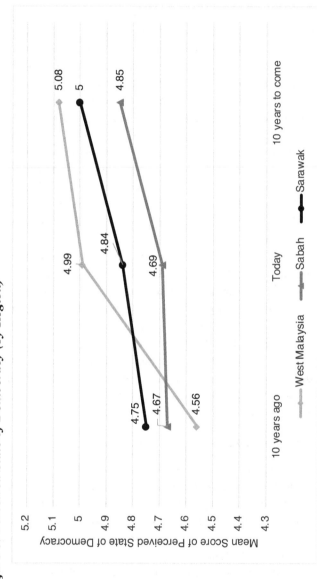

significant vote swing had led to a historic change of federal government, it might have contributed to the perceived improvement in the state of democracy among West Malaysians who had voted for change. On the other hand, for a significant section of Sarawakians who seemed to be satisfied with the status quo and did not express a desire for political change, the default disposition was moderately positive and expectant of gradual improvement. As for Sabah, there was an indication that the electoral losses suffered by PH and Warisan during the state election were in part due to voter disappointment with the outgoing PH Plus state government's performance (Welsh 2020; Chung 2020). The 2020 state election which had subsequently led to the serious spread of COVID-19 infections in the state would also have left a bitter taste among Sabahans towards politicians. From their point of view, political development since GE14 had not brought about any radical improvement to their daily lives; hence their negative sentiment when assessing the state of democracy, as well as other indicators that will be discussed shortly.

When analysed based on the extent of urbanization of the location (Figure 9), we see that semi-urban residents express a greater appreciation of the extent of democratization in the country over the last 10 years and have the highest aspiration for its improvement in the 10 years to come. The rural folks, on the other hand, perceive minimal improvement in democracy over the last 10 years and do not have high expectation for the next 10 years either. Being the most critical of the state of democracy a decade back, urban residents perceive the greatest progress being made thus far, though they have a moderate expectation of its amelioration in the decade to come.

(b) Satisfaction with the State of Civil Liberties

When compared with the appreciation of the state of democracy, the level of satisfaction vis-à-vis the more specific aspects of civil liberties appears to be lower. Except for the freedom of association, the median values for media freedom, freedom of expression and assembly drop to 4 (Table 8). Freedom of assembly is considered the least satisfactory dimension among the four.

When compared by region (Figure 10), Sabahans again emerge clearly as the least satisfied lot, and perceive the state of media freedom

Figure 9: Perceived State of Democracy (Urban/Rural)

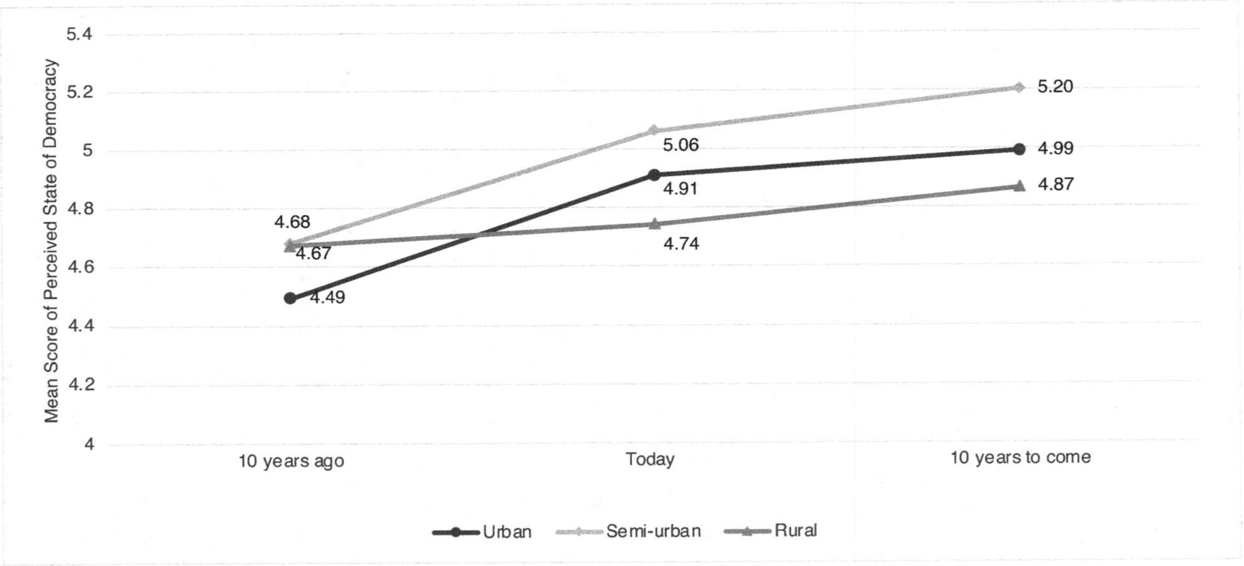

29

Table 8: Satisfaction with the State of Civil Liberties

On a scale of 1 to 7, please indicate your level of satisfaction with the political situations and democracy in our country *(1 signifies "very dissatisfied" and 7 signifies "very satisfied").*					
	N	**Mean**	**Median**	**Mode**	**Std. Dev.**
Media freedom	2,627	4.42	4	5	1.288
Freedom of expression	2,627	4.44	4	4	1.286
Freedom of association	2,627	4.61	5	5	1.277
Freedom of assembly	2,627	4.36	4	4	1.293

as the least satisfactory. Sarawakians, on the other hand, express the highest level of satisfaction vis-à-vis media freedom among the three regions. All three regions regard the freedom of association as the most satisfactory among the four civil liberties.

A comparison of the perception of residents in locations with a different degree of urbanization (Figure 11) found that urban Malaysians are the least satisfied with all the four dimensions of freedom. Nonetheless, the state of freedom of association again is regarded as the most satisfied dimension among the four. Interestingly, when the average values of the mean scores of the four dimensions of freedom are compared, it is the semi-urban residents who are the most satisfied group among the three.

TRUST IN AND SATISFACTION WITH STATE INSTITUTIONS

In our analysis of public trust in and satisfaction with political authorities, we distinguish between those state institutions which are supposedly "neutral" politically and "partisan" institutions such as the parliament and the cabinet, i.e., political bodies which are formed based on the outcomes of partisan choices made by citizens in a general election. The five non-partisan institutions included in this survey are the judiciary, the civil service, Royal Malaysia Police (PDRM), the MACC and the EC. For the level of satisfaction with performance, the respondents were

Figure 10: Satisfaction with the State of Civil Liberties (by Region)

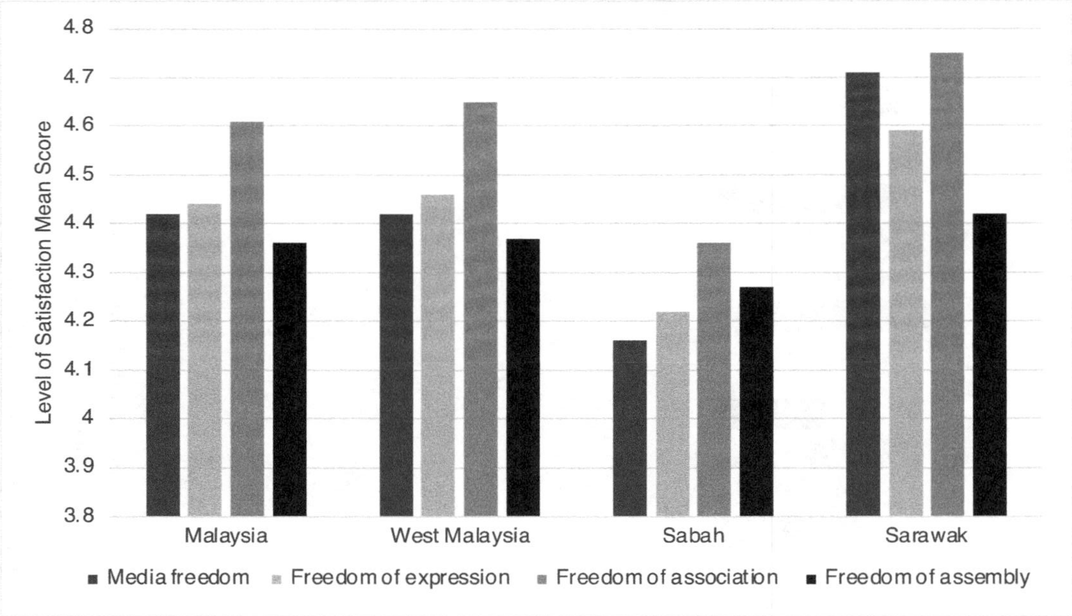

Figure 11: Satisfaction with the State of Civil Liberties (Urban/Rural)

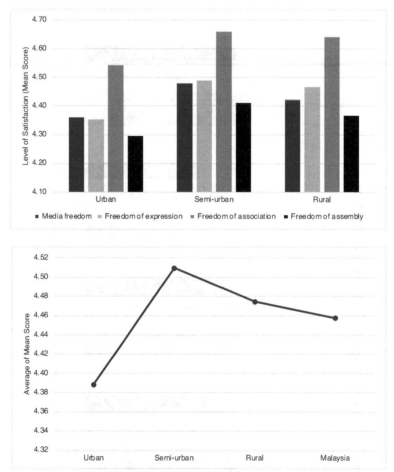

only asked to rate their level of satisfaction with the cabinet, government backbenchers and opposition parliamentarians.

(a) Trust in Non-Partisan Political Authorities

Mean scores of trust indicated by respondents on various non-partisan state institutions hover around 4.6 and both median and mode values are 5 on a scale of 7 (see Figure 12 and Table 9). This indicates that a great number of Malaysians oscillate between the sceptical attitude at 4 and a conservative "pass" of 5 in terms of trust in the non-partisan state institutions—a weak expression of trust. Notable for our purpose here is that Malaysians express a similar level of trust towards all the five non-partisan state authorities. On the other hand, when compared with their rating of civil liberties, Malaysians appear to be slightly more positive towards non-partisan state authorities.

A comparison of the mean scores by region (see Figure 13) shows Sarawakians having the highest level of trust in the integrity and transparency of all five institutions. Notable differences between West Malaysians and Sabahans are that while they almost coincide in their trust in the police force, Sabahans express the lowest trust towards the judiciary and the civil service, while West Malaysians express notable distrust towards MACC and the EC.

A comparison between respondents residing in locations with different degree of urbanization (Figure 14) found that urban residents consistently express greater mistrust towards all five state institutions. Rural residents, on the other hand, register higher confidence in them across the board.

Table 9: Trust in Non-Partisan Institutions

On a scale of 1 to 7, please indicate your level of trust towards the following institutions in terms of transparency and integrity in carrying out their responsibilities *(1 signifies "strongly distrust" and 7 signifies "trust fully")*

	N	Mean	Median	Mode	Std. Dev.
Judiciary	2,627	4.62	5	5	1.299
Civil Service	2,627	4.65	5	5	1.243
PDRM	2,627	4.65	5	5	1.365
MACC	2,627	4.63	5	5	1.346
EC	2,627	4.65	5	5	1.360

Figure 12: Trust in Transparency and Integrity of Non-partisan Institutions
(1 = strongly distrust, 7 = trust fully)

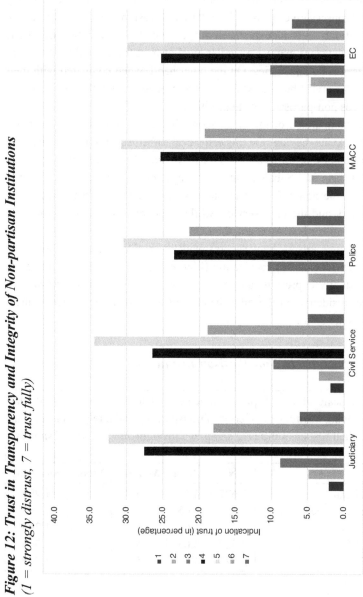

Figure 13: Trust in Integrity and Transparency of Non-partisan Institutions (Regional Comparison)

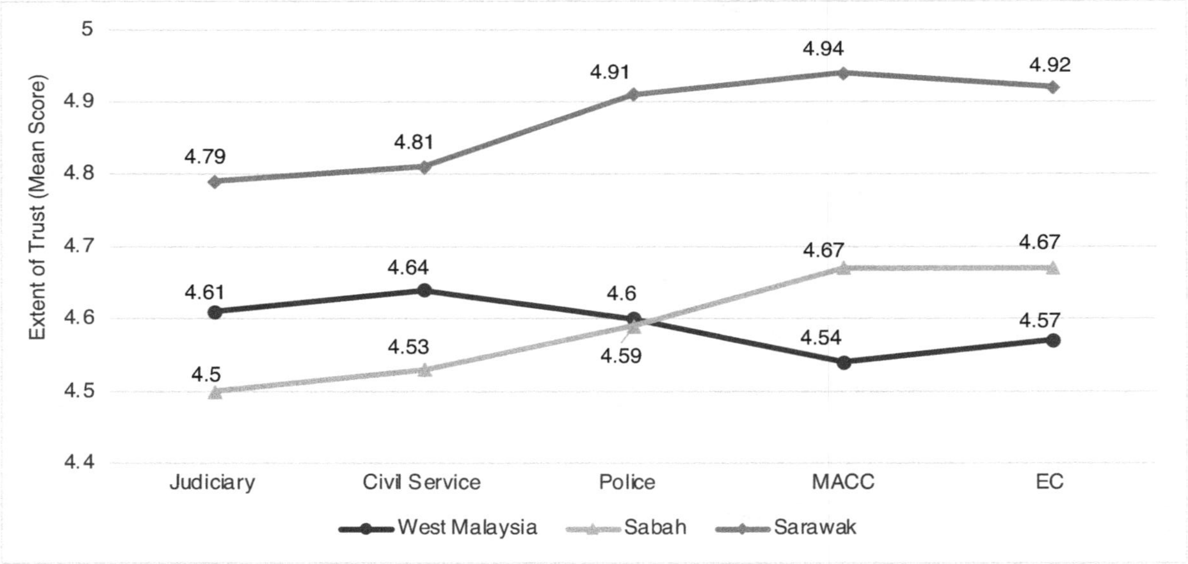

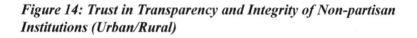

Figure 14: Trust in Transparency and Integrity of Non-partisan Institutions (Urban/Rural)

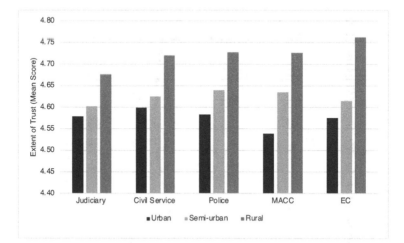

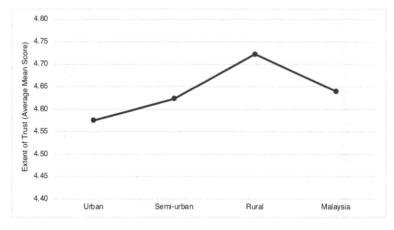

Table 10: Trust in Partisan Institutions

On a scale of 1 to 7, please indicate your level of trust towards the following institutions in terms of transparency and integrity in carrying out their responsibilities *(1 signifies "strongly distrust" and 7 signifies "trust fully")*					
	N	**Mean**	**Median**	**Mode**	**Std. Dev.**
Executive (Cabinet)	2,627	4.43	5	5	1.263
Parliament	2,627	4.46	5	5	1.264

(b) Trust in Partisan Institutions

When compared with the non-partisan institutions, Malaysians appear to have less trust in the transparency and integrity of the parliament and cabinet in carrying out their responsibilities as indicated by the lower mean scores (Table 10).

A notable regional difference here is the markedly lower trust in parliament and the cabinet expressed by Sabahans (see Figure 15). While West Malaysians and Sabahans express a greater trust in the parliament than the cabinet, Sarawakians stand out in placing higher trust in the cabinet than in the parliament. As in the case of non-partisan state authorities, urban residents again express much lower trust compared with semi-urban and rural folks, in the Executive and the parliament. Semi-urban residents place markedly higher trust in the parliament while rural residents place a higher trust in the cabinet.

(c) Satisfaction with the Performance of Partisan Institutions

Respondents are also asked to rate their satisfaction with the performance of partisan institutions, namely, the cabinet, the ruling parliamentarians and the opposition parliamentarians. It is notable that the median and mode values for the performance of both the cabinet and the opposition parliamentarians drop to 4, while the standard deviation indicates a greater dispersion than the confidence rating for the partisan institutions

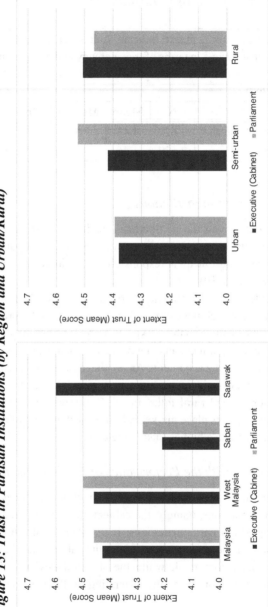

Figure 15: Trust in Partisan Institutions (by Region and Urban/Rural)

Table 11: Satisfaction with the Performance of Partisan Institutions

On a scale of 1 to 7, please indicate your level of satisfaction with the political situations and democracy in our country *(1 signifies "very dissatisfied" and 7 signifies "very satisfied")*.					
	N	**Mean**	**Median**	**Mode**	**Std. Dev.**
Performance of the cabinet	2,627	4.39	4	4	1.340
Performance of ruling parliamentarians	2,627	4.48	5	5	1.326
Performance of opposition parliamentarians	2,627	4.42	4	4	1.326

(Table 11). This could be due to the specificity of the subjects being evaluated, i.e., the linkage to the immediate political reality in the country and the divisive effects of partisanship among the respondents. As a whole, the performance of the cabinet is rated as the least satisfactory among the three, while the ruling people's representatives are rated slightly more satisfactorily than for the opposition.

A regional comparison (see Figure 16) again reveals that Sabahans feel the least satisfied with the performance of the partisan institutions. Sarawakians, on the other hand, express the highest level of satisfaction with the performance of the cabinet and the ruling parliamentarians among the three regions. Sarawakians notably express unhappiness with the performance of opposition parliamentarians.

Respondents living in locations with different degrees of urbanization display intriguing variations in terms of their appreciation of the performance of partisan institutions (Figure 16). While urban dwellers unsurprisingly indicate the lowest level of satisfaction, rural dwellers express stronger dissatisfaction than semi-urban residents towards the performance of the partisan institutions as a whole (note the average mean score value). Rural residents nonetheless express markedly higher

Figure 16: Satisfaction with Performance of Partisan Institutions (by Region and Urban/Rural)

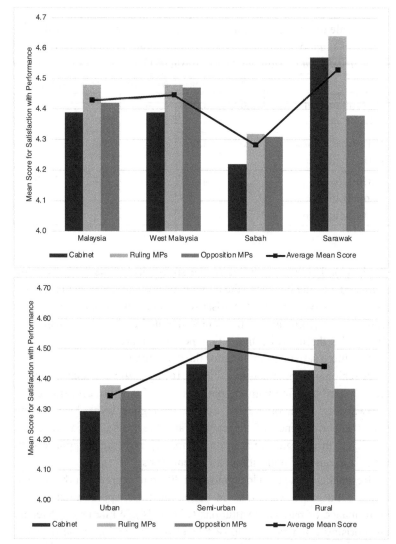

satisfaction with the performance of the ruling parliamentarians, though the mean score has a higher value of standard deviation, indicating that their views as a group are more divergent than for the urban or semi-urban dwellers collectively.

As is evident in Figure 17, it is clear that Malaysians place a higher level of confidence in non-partisan institutions than in partisan ones. This is consistent both across the regions and transcends the rural-urban divide.

Figure 17: Trust in Institutions (by Region and Urban/Rural)

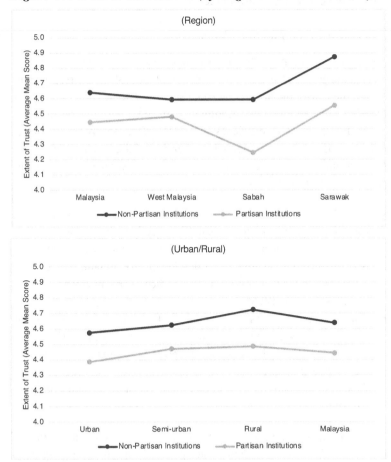

PERCEPTION OF THE ELECTION COMMISSION AND THE MANAGEMENT OF ELECTIONS

The survey asked respondents a range of questions related to the functions performed by the EC at the various stages of the electoral process, in maintaining the electoral roll and with regard to the electoral constituency delineation. They were also asked whether they thought the last general election in 2018 (GE14), and the Sabah state election in 2020, were conducted freely and fairly.

Perception of the Election Commission

Two sets of questions on how the various aspects of the electoral process were managed by the EC were posed. One set asked the respondents to rate their level of satisfaction (on a scale of 1 to 7, with 1 signifying the least satisfied and 7 as "absolutely satisfied") with the performance of the EC in terms of efficiency and professionalism. A second set of questions asked them to rate their perception of the extent to which the EC was impartial and free from partisan politics when managing the same aspects of the electoral process:

- The Election Commission of Malaysia (EC) is an agency responsible for administering matters related to elections in Malaysia. On a scale of 1 to 7, please indicate your level of satisfaction with their performance in managing the following electoral matters in terms of *efficiency and professionalism.* (1 signifies "very dissatisfied" and 7 signifies "very satisfied".)
- The Election Commission of Malaysia (EC) is an agency responsible for administering matters related to elections in Malaysia. On a scale of 1 to 7, please indicate your perception of the extent to which the EC is *free from the influence of party politics* with regard to the following electoral matters. (1 signifies "very unfree" and 7 signifies "absolutely free".)

The respective appraisals of the same set of items in terms of professionalism and freedom from political interference appear to be correlated, replicating a similar pattern in terms of appreciation (Figure 18). Among the different functions and processes operated by the EC, the one aspect which stands out for both sets of questions is the notably lower mean score in the administration of the constituency delineation exercise. In effect, the median and mode values of the answers on all electoral aspects for both sets of questions are consistently 5 on a scale of 7 except for the perceived political neutrality in performing boundary delimitation whose mode value is 4.

In other words, Malaysians generally perceive the constituency delimitation as performed by the EC as the least free from the influence of party politics, as well as the least professionally executed by the EC when compared with its other responsibilities. The processes of vote counting and postal voting are also regarded as the lesser satisfactory from the point of view of efficiency and professionalism as well as impartiality from the influence of party politics. The performance of election officials, on the other hand, are perceived as the most satisfactory in terms of efficiency and professionalism in executing their duties.

A slightly different picture emerges when comparing regional perceptions (Figure 19). Contrary to other regions, Sabahans do not particularly appreciate the role played by the election officials in terms of performance and political impartiality when compared with other electoral matters. They are also the most dissatisfied with the performance of the EC vis-à-vis the voting process, the monitoring of the election campaigns and the vote counting process. Sarawak appears the most satisfied with EC's performance and the most trusting in the political neutrality of the EC. West Malaysians are the most particular in their evaluation of the performance in various aspects of election management by the EC, and in their assessment of EC's freedom from partisan politics.

In terms of the urban-rural divide (Figure 20), rural residents express greater satisfaction with the EC's performance as well as greater confidence that they carry out their duties free from partisan politics. On the other hand, the urban and semi-urban dwellers appear to share similar views on their evaluation of the performance of the EC; however, urban Malaysians express lower trust in the political neutrality of the EC than do the semi-urban dwellers.

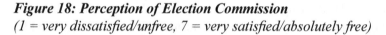

Figure 18: Perception of Election Commission
(1 = very dissatisfied/unfree, 7 = very satisfied/absolutely free)

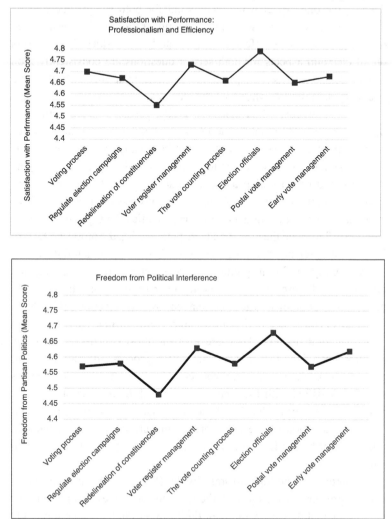

Figure 19: Perception of Election Commission (by Region)
(1 = very dissatisfied/unfree, 7 = very satisfied/absolutely free)

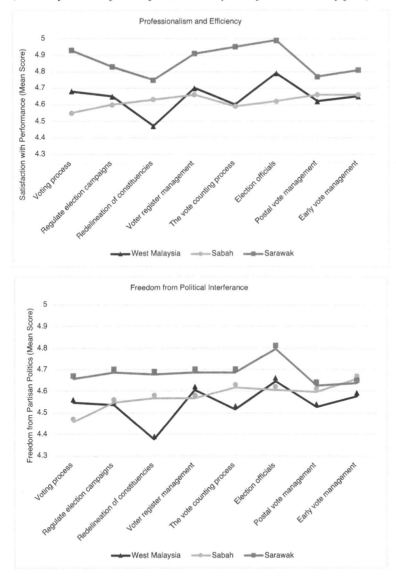

Figure 20: Perception of Election Commission (Urban/Rural)

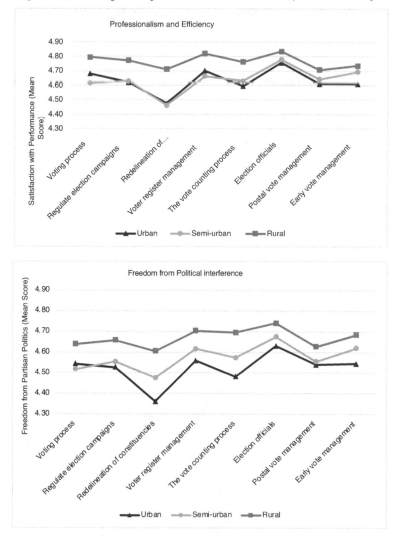

Figure 21 compares the perception of professionalism and political impartiality for each region, and based on the extent of urbanization. Again, it is clear that the assessment of both dimensions is correlated. Notable is that trust in the political neutrality of the EC is manifestly less when compared with satisfaction with its performance of duties. The average score for the overall efficiency and professionalism of the EC in exercising its various functions is 4.68 while its perceived political impartiality is 4.59.

The results from a separate question on online voting also confirm this lack of trust in the EC (Figure 22). The respondents were asked if Malaysia implements an online voting system, how confident they were that it would be conducted transparently. 54 per cent of the respondents indicated that they were "not confident" or have "very low confidence", while 26.7 per cent said that they were "unsure". In effect, this worry was also expressed by many in the last open-ended question asking them to share any suggestions for electoral reform. About 10 per cent of the responses expressed concern about holding elections during the pandemic. Around one third among these responses supported online voting while two thirds urged to wait till the pandemic was under control and even then, to do it with strict preventive SOPs in place.

Respondents were asked whether they observed any difference in the independence of the EC before and after the last general election. About 49 per cent responded that they were "unsure", while only about 25 per cent said that it was "very different" or "different" (Figure 23).

Appraisal of Past Elections

When asked whether the last general election which was held in 2018 (GE14) was free or fair (in two separate questions), around 67 per cent of the respondents either thought that it was "fair/free" or "fair/free with some other problems" (see Figure 24). Less than 7 per cent of the respondents thought that the 2018 general election was not fairly or freely held. On the other hand, about 26 per cent felt unsure or do not know whether the general election was held freely or fairly.

Who were these more than a quarter of the respondents who responded that they were unsure or did not know whether GE14 was

Figure 21: Overall Perception of Election Commission (by Region and Urban/Rural)

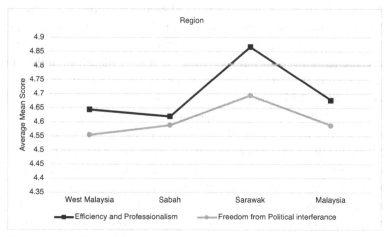

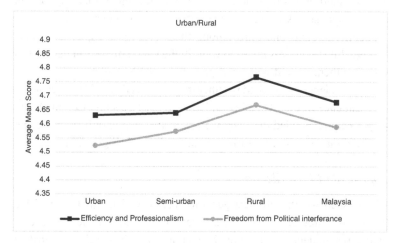

Figure 22: If Malaysia Switches to an Online Voting System, What Is Your Level of Confidence That It Will Be Conducted Transparently?

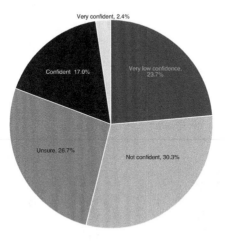

Figure 23: Perception of the Independence of the EC Before and After the 2018 General Election

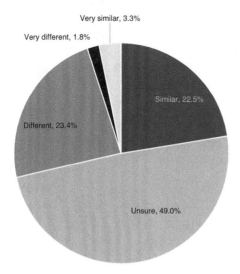

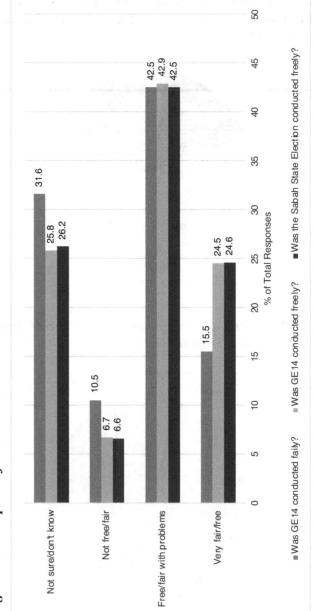

Figure 24: Perception of Past Elections

held freely or fairly? One plausible answer could be that many of them belonged to the youngest cohort of respondents and felt that they were not informed enough to judge because they had not voted or registered themselves as voters. When their responses were cross-tabulated against their age, it was found that about 40 per cent of them are aged 25 years old or less. When tabulated against the number of times they had voted (see Table 12), 55.8 per cent of them had not registered as a voter or had registered but not voted. In the focus group discussions with participants at the age range of 24 years old or younger, it was found that some of them said that because they had never voted before or were young then, they were unsure whether GE14 was conducted in a clean and fair manner.

Another explanation for why some respondents chose this response was that they were disinterested in or uninformed about the country's political development. When cross-tabulated against the frequency with which they followed news about politics, about 80 per cent fell into the categories of those who either read political news once or twice per week or not at all. Hence it is likely that many of these respondents were not engaged or concerned with the current politics of the country.

The respondents were also asked whether they saw the 2020 Sabah state election as being held freely. 58 per cent responded either that it was a free election or "free though with some other problems". On the other hand, those who thought that the state election was not held freely increased to 10.5 per cent, and 31.6 per cent responded that they were unsure or "don't know". Here again, when cross-tabulated against their frequency in following political news, 71 per cent of them fall into the categories of those who either read such news once or twice a week or not at all. In effect, almost two thirds of those who responded that they were "unsure or don't know" either had not registered as a voter, or had registered but never voted, or only voted once.

The consistent pattern that emerges from Figure 24 is that slightly more than 40 per cent of the respondents perceived both elections as free and fair but had problems. About a quarter regarded the 2018 general election as "very free" or "very fair" but less so for the 2020 Sabah state election. Hence it was not an unqualified endorsement and there was widespread recognition that some aspects of these elections were "problematic". In our questionnaire, we had included a follow-up

Table 12: Perception of the Conduct of GE14

How many times have you voted in an election?	Was GE14 conducted fairly?				Total (status as voter)
	Very fair	Fair but there are other problems	Not fair	Not sure/ don't know	
Once	95	195	30	83	403
Twice	102	144	32	78	356
Three times	71	134	21	53	279
Four times	34	61	9	22	126
More than 4 times	141	261	36	69	507
Registered but never voted	86	125	16	103	330
Not registered yet	118	197	30	281	626
Total	647	1,117	174	689	2,627

open-ended question asking the respondents to provide reasons for their responses. Most did not respond and after eliminating responses such as "don't know", "not sure", etc, 250 responses (9.5 per cent) remained, which can be meaningfully categorised, as indicated in Table 13.

The first category of answers, mostly among those who said that GE14 was free or fair but not exclusively, stated that the election was conducted in accordance with the principle of fairness or with the right procedure. They consist of short answers such as "*adil, saksama*" (fair, equitable), "*tidak berat sebelah*" (not biased), "*kerana semua parti bebas bertanding*" (because all the parties were free to contest), "*tak de masalah*" (no problem), "*semua berjalan dengan lancar dan sebaiknya*" (all went smoothly and it was as best as could be), "*sebab ada ketelusan*" (because there was transparency).

The second type of answers among those who responded that GE14 was free or fair, can be summarized as those who thought that since there was a change in government, it must have been fair or free, and gave candid answers such as, "*Najib kalah*" (Najib lost), or a more elaborate one such as "*kalau Datuk Najib sebagai Perdana Menteri boleh kalah, ini bermaksud SPR tidak berlaku bohong dalam undian*" (if Datuk Najib as the Prime Minister could be defeated, it means that the EC did not cheat in the election). There were also those who reasoned that the power

Table 13: Rationale Given in Answer to Whether GE14 Was Free and Fair

	Response	Count	Percentage (%)
1.	Followed the right procedure/principle	77	30.8
2.	"We managed to change the government"	37	14.8
3.	Election management issues	84	33.6
4.	Suspicion	21	8.4
5.	Post-election grouses	31	12.4
	Total	250	100

transition happened peacefully, or emphasized that the people were able to choose a government based on what they wanted. A sampling of these answers is as follows: *"peralihan kuasa berlangsung dengan baik"* (power transition happened well), *"berlaku pertukaran kerajaan"* (a change of government took place), *"rakyat mengubah kerajaan asal menggunakan hak mereka"* (people exercised their right to change the incumbent government), *"kalau tidak adil, kerajaan terdahulu tidak akan melepaskan kuasa"* (if not fair, the previous government would not have conceded defeat), *"kerana melalui pilihan raya rakyat bebas memilih pemimpin dengan adil"* (through the election, the people were free to choose their leaders fairly).

A third category of responses are consisted of complaints related to specific aspects of the electoral process such as vote buying, dirty tactics being used, political interference, defective postal voting and vote counting, including references to the delays in the announcement of the results.

A fourth category of responses simply expressed suspicion that something was amiss but did not give any specific complaints against the election management process. One said *"ada masalah tetapi saya kurang pasti"* (there are problems but I am not sure); and another said, "my parents say *ada banyak rasuah*" (my parents said that there was a lot of corruption). The last category of responses refers to "problems" unrelated to the conduct of elections. They expressed dissatisfaction about party hopping, as well as political manoeuvrings by politicians.

To end this section, the following thoughts shared by a Malay middle-class person in the Klang Valley in a focus group discussion characterize the ambivalence of some of the respondents. It expressed a lack of trust while giving reserved approval:

Penilaian tadbir urus pilihan raya, dia menguruskan pilihan raya tu macam mana ... Technically, yang saya nampak, okay, dia punya pengurusan tu, boleh saya kata tak sangat memuaskan, tapi masih lagi memuaskanlah ... technically, sistem pengurusan dia tu. Cuma yang saya cakap tadi, yang belakang-belakang tu kita tak tahulah macam mana, kan? Samaada ada pengundi hantu ke, tak ada pengundi hantu ke, hah itu perkara yang kedua. Sebab kalau kita tengok dari segi apa yang kita perlu fokus, penilaian tadbir urus pilihan raya di Malaysia: technically, pandangan saya dia punya tu, memuaskanlah buat masa sekarang ni. Okay? Dan bila kita tengok sistem pilihan raya kita ni, ya masih ada loophole untuk kita perbaiki, okay.

(To evaluate the administration of election and how it was managed ... Technically, what I see is, okay, its management was not very satisfactory, but still satisfactory *lah*.... technically, it's the management system. But as I said just now, we don't know what happened behind the scene, right? Whether there were phantom voters or not, hah, that is another story. Because we only focus on the evaluation of the administration of election in Malaysia: technically, my view is that it's satisfactory for the time being. Okay? And if we look at our electoral system, yes, there are still loopholes that we can improve on, okay.)

CONCLUSIONS

This survey explores perceptions Malaysians have of the EC and of matters related to election management. It does so by contextualizing these perceptions within the larger framework of perspectives on democracy, civil liberties and state institutions. Political scientists have observed that interpreting concepts such as political support and legitimacy requires that attention be paid to different layers of meaning at which they may be understood and the temporal nature of support. Hence, we have introduced the notions of "diffuse support" as distinguished from "specific support" on two extremes of a continuum in our conceptual framework. The political objects to which the support was directed range from the more abstract such as democratic principles, state institutions or authorities to the more specific such as government and the parliament of the day. Distinction is also made between the more changeable notion of satisfaction with the performance of the political object and the more stable feeling of trust towards it. Perceptions of the workings of the EC and public trust in it may be understood in that light, between the more changeable and specific partisan institutions such as the cabinet or parliament and the more general, stable and supposedly non-partisan state authorities such as the judiciary, the civil service or the police. In addition, we have also noted that public perception and political support as a subjective phenomenon should be distinguished from an objective assessment based on normative ideals.

Based on the survey findings, Malaysians by and large expressed a cautious, moderate affirmation of the state of democracy in Malaysia. The fact that the last general election had brought about a change in the federal government seems to have contributed to that perspective. They also think that the state of democracy will improve in the decade to come, even though only very slightly and not as much as the progress made over the past decade. When asked to evaluate the more specific and immediate dimensions of civil liberty, the assessment became less upbeat and variable, depending on the civil liberty concerned.

There are interesting regional variations in this perception of the state of democracy. West Malaysians appear to be on both extremes in their assessment, giving the worst assessment of the past and the best for the present and future states of democracy. Sabahans feel that the improvement in the state of democracy thus far has been slight, and hence they have lower expectation of what the next decade holds. The level of satisfaction with various civil liberties is also markedly lower than in other regions. Sarawakians are situated in the middle in their assessment of the state of democracy, but expressed the highest level of satisfaction toward the exercise of civil liberties.

Rural Malaysians interestingly returned the lowest assessment of the state of democracy in Malaysia. Semi-urban dwellers are the most positive about both the state of democracy and satisfaction with the state of civil liberties. Urban Malaysians expressed the least satisfaction with the space for civil liberties. In this sense, West Malaysians and urbanites appear to resemble the notion of "critical citizens", while Sarawakians and rural dwellers seem to project a political disposition of conformism and compliance within a more authoritarian or hierarchical environment. The latter observation was offered by a politician from Sarawak in reaction to the findings, which corresponds with the impression obtained in focus group discussions with the rural poor in Sarawak. The fact that a much higher proportion of Sarawakian respondents relied on television as one of their main channels in accessing political news and current affairs may also have shaped their more pro-establishment attitude. Yet this explanation seems to be contradicted by the findings on Sabahan respondents whose perspectives depart largely from those from Sarawak.

We also found that Malaysians have a higher level of trust in non-partisan state authorities such as the judiciary, the civil service, the police, the MACC and the EC than the partisan ones such as the cabinet or the parliament. Even so, this expression of trust hovers between scepticism (score of 4 on a scale of 7) and the reserved approval of 5. The fragility of the confidence in the EC is demonstrated by responses to the question how confident they were that the implementation of an online voting system would be conducted transparently. By region, Sarawakians expressed the highest level of trust in both partisan and non-partisan state institutions. Sabahans again expressed the lowest level of trust in both partisan and non-partisan state authorities, except for the MACC and the EC. West Malaysians stand out in their distrust for the MACC and the EC, the latter in particular in terms of their lack of freedom from partisan politics.

Rural Malaysians hold all state authorities in high regard in terms of trust and professionalism. Urban Malaysians are the most distrustful of and dissatisfied with the EC, and the least satisfied with the performance of partisan state institutions.

With regard to the EC, the public generally have a more positive assessment of its professionalism and efficiency than trust in its political impartiality. As we have noted, two-thirds of the respondents either stated that they "never" followed news related to politics and government or just "once or twice per week". This suggests a scenario where three quarters of Malaysians do not have enough information to evaluate the performance of the EC or are well read enough about current affairs to notice various reform measures taken to improve its service delivery during the by-elections. Only about a quarter could evaluate correctly the veracity of the three statements made on the power of the EC and on the conditions for the appointment of its chairperson. Hence it is perhaps unsurprising that most respondents seem to perceive the EC from some distance, in a similar light as they perceive other non-partisan state institutions.

While the standing of the EC is comparable to other non-partisan state institutions in the public eye, one notable consensus is their less favourable evaluation of the EC in carrying out boundary delimitation. This is likely due to the contentious constituency delimitation exercise that was concluded just before the last general election, and which was pushed through despite public objections of it. It is important for measures to be taken to ensure the political independence of the EC in order to further improve public confidence in it. In addition, it is important that the EC have more public engagement and communicate to the public the reform agenda that it has been carrying out.

ACKNOWLEDGEMENT

This study is made possible by the generous support of the United States Agency for International Development (USAID). However, the authors are solely responsible for the contents of the report, which do not necessarily reflect the views of USAID, the United States Government, or DAI Global LLC. The authors also wish to acknowledge the hard work and dedication of Vyshnav Menon N.P. Prem Kumar and Randy Ho Xu Zhe who have assisted tirelessly in the gathering of information, preparation of graphs, tables and the formatting of the report.

REFERENCES

BERSIH 2.0. 2018. *Media Statement (23 May 2018): New Government Must Act Immediately to Restore Public Confidence in the Election Commission.*

Chacko, Danesh Prakash. 2019. "Winning Elections by Rigging Borders? Barisan Nasional's Brazen, and Failed, Attempt". In *The Defeat of Barisan Nasional: Missed Signs or Late Surge?* edited by Francis E. Hutchinson and Lee Hwok Aun, pp. 49–84. Singapore: ISEAS – Yusof Ishak Institute.

Chang, Alex, Chu Yun-han and Bridget Welsh. 2013. "Southeast Asia: Sources of Regime Support". *Journal of Democracy* 24, no. 2: 150–64.

Chu, Yun-han, and Bridget Welsh. 2015. "Millennials and East Asia's Democratic Future". *Journal of Democracy* 26, no. 2: 151–64.

Chu, Yun-han, Bridget Welsh and Alex Chang. 2013. "Congruence and Variation in Sources of Regime Support in East Asia". *Taiwan Journal of Democracy* 9, no. 1: 221–37.

Chung, Nicolas. 2020. 'BN Support Shifting to PN, Survey Finds". *Free Malaysia Today*, 25 September 2020.

Easton, David. 1975. "A Re-assessment of the Concept of Political Support". *British Journal of Political Science* 5, no. 4: 435–57.

Fann, Thomas. 2019. "Malaysia Begins Rectifying Major Flaws in its Election System". ISEAS *Perspective*, no. 2019/55, 12 July 2019.

Huang, Kai-ping, Lee Feng-yu and Lin Tse-min. 2013. "Partisanship and Institutional Trust: A Comparative Analysis of Emerging Democracies in East Asia". *Taiwan Journal of Democracy* 9, no. 1: 47–71.

Huang, Min-Hua, Chu Yun-han and Chang Yu-tzung. 2013. "Popular Understandings of Democracy and Regime Legitimacy in East Asia". *Taiwan Journal of Democracy* 9, no. 1: 147–71.

Ikeda, Ken'ichi. 2013. "Social and Institutional Trust in East and Southeast Asia". *Taiwan Journal of Democracy* 9, no. 1: 13–45.

Kang, Youngho, and Lee Dongwon. 2018. "Delegative Democratic Attitudes: Theory and Evidence from the Asian Barometer Survey". *International Political Science Review* 39, no. 4: 455–72.

Kotzian, Peter. 2011. "Public Support for Liberal Democracy". *International Political Science Review* 32, no. 1: 23–41.

Levitsky, Steven, and Lucan Way. 2010. *Competitive Authoritarianism: Hybrid Regimes after the Cold War*. Cambridge: Cambridge University Press.

Lim Hong Hai. 2002. "Electoral Politics in Malaysia: 'Managing' Elections in a Plural Society". In *Electoral Politics in Southeast Asia and East Asia*, edited by Aurel Croissant, pp. 101–48. Singapore: Friedrich Ebert Stiftung.

———. 2005. "Making the System Work: the Election Commission". In *Elections and Democracy in Malaysia*, edited by Mavis Puthucheary and Norani Othman, pp. 249–91. Bangi: Penerbit UKM.

Mohd Nor, Mohd Roslan, and Ahmad Mahmud. 2013. "The Malay Muslim Dilemma in Malaysia after the 12th General Election". *Malaysian Journal of Democracy and Election Studies* 1, no. 1: 10–23.

Muhammad Fathi Yusof et al. 2015. "Public Perception towards the Election Commission in Malaysia". *Asian Social Science* 11, no. 26: 347–57.

Mujani, Saiful, and R. William Liddle. 2013. "Generational Change, Political Institutions, and Regime Support in East Asia". *Taiwan Journal of Democracy* 9, no. 1: 173–97.

Norris, Pippa. 2011. *Democratic Deficit: Critical Citizens Revisited.* Cambridge University Press.

Park, Chong-Min. 2013. "Democratic Quality of Institutions and Regime Support in East Asia". *Taiwan Journal of Democracy* 9, no. 1: 93–116.

PEMANTAU. 2018. *Election Observation Report of the 14th Malaysian General Election.* Petaling Jaya: Bersih and Adil Network Sdn Bhd.

Rachagan, S. Sothi. 1993. *Law and the Electoral Process.* Kuala Lumpur: University of Malaya Press.

Wang, Zhengxu, and Tan Ern Ser. 2013. "The Conundrum of Authoritarian Resiliency: Hybrid and Nondemocratic Regimes in East Asia". *Taiwan Journal of Democracy* 9, no. 1: 199–219.

Welsh, Bridget. 1996. "Attitudes Towards Democracy in Malaysia: Challenges to the Regime". *Asian Survey* 36, no. 9: 882–903.

———. 2014. *Malaysia: Political Polarization in a Hybrid Regime.* ABS Working Paper Series, No. 106. http://www.asianbarometer.org/publications/abs-working-paper-series (accessed 13 May 2021).

———. 2020. 'Comment | Why Warisan Plus Lost—A Preliminary Analysis". *Malaysiakini*, 28 September 2020.

———, Ibrahim Suffian and Andrew Aeria. 2007. *Malaysia Country Report: Second Wave of Asian Barometer Survey.* ABS Working Paper Series, No. 46. http://www.asianbarometer.org/publications/abs-working-paper-series (accessed 13 May 2021).

———, Ibrahim Suffian and Andrew Aeria. 2008. "The State of Democracy in Malaysia: Public Perceptions". Working paper presented at the Asian Barometer Conference on the State of Democratic Governance in Asia, 20–21 June 2008 (ABS Conference Paper, No. 09). http://www.asianbarometer.org/publications/the-asian-barometer-conference-on-the-state-of-democratic-governance-in-asia-june-20-21-2008-taipei (accessed 12 May 2021).